ATOMIC

FIGHTER PILOT

JAMESON ANDERSON

Raintree

Chicago, Illinois

Printed in China by WKT

11 10 09 08 07
10 9 8 7 6 5 4 3 2 1

**Library of Congress Cataloging-in-
Publication Data**
Anderson, Jameson.
  Fighter pilot / Jameson Anderson.
    p. cm. -- (Atomic)
  Includes bibliographical references and index.
  ISBN 1-4109-2496-3 (library binding-hardcover)
-- ISBN 1-4109-2501-3 (pbk.)
  1. Aeronautics, Military--Juvenile literature. 2.
Fighter pilots--Juvenile literature. 3. Airplanes--
Piloting--Juvenile literature. 4. Airplanes, Military-
-Juvenile literature. I. Title. II. Series: Atomic
(Chicago, Ill.)

UG631.A52 2006
623.74'64--dc22

     2006002928

13 digit ISBNs:
978-1-4109-2496-4 (hardcover)
978-1-4109-2501-5 (paperback)

Acknowledgments
The author and publishers are grateful to the
following for permission to reproduce copyright
material: Corbis pp. **5**, **12**, **20 top** and **bottom**,
24 (George Hall), **6** (Jim Richardson), **17** (Philip
Wallick); Defense Visual Information Centre
p. **19 bottom**; Empics/AP p. **27**; Getty/Time & Life
Pictures p. **9**; Getty Images/USAF p. **11**; Lockheed
Martin pp. **14 bottom**, **19 top**, **28**; Sanford/
Agliolo/Corbis p. **14 top**; Topham/Photri p. **23**.

Cover photograph reproduced with permission of
Corbis (Philip Wallick).

The publishers would like to thank Diana Bentley,
Nancy Harris, and Dee Reid for their assistance in
the preparation of this book.

Every effort has been made to contact copyright
holders of any material reproduced in this book.
Any omissions will be rectified in subsequent
printings if notice is given to the publishers.

Contents

Some words are printed in bold, **like this.** You can find out what they mean in the glossary. You can also look in the box at the bottom of the page where the word first appears.

LIFE IN THE SKY

Fighter pilots have one of the most exciting jobs in the military. They respond at a moment's notice to attacks, threats, and scares anywhere in the world.

What do fighter pilots do?

The most important job of a fighter pilot is to protect the skies and to stop enemy aircraft from attacking us. Sometimes, if enemy forces attack our soldiers, the military sends fighter pilots to protect them. If they have to, fighter pilots attack the enemy forces. They can bomb buildings and shoot at vehicles.

Fighter fact!

An F-15 Eagle can climb to a height of 30,000ft (9km) in about a minute.

military   group of soldiers that fight to protect a country

F–15 Eagles and an F/A–18 Hornet (left) fly over an enemy area to show the military's strength.

Training improves both physical and mental strength.

TRAINING TIME

Before fighter pilots in the U.S. Air Force can take a seat in a plane, they go through tough training.

Why do pilots train?

Fighter pilots in training must exercise and build muscle. They need to be fit to spend time in a fighter plane. This is because speeds of 1,500 miles (2,400 kilometers) per hour put a great pressure on the body. Pilots also need to be mentally fit, so they can think very carefully about what they are doing for long periods of time.

Fighter fact!

More than 36,000 people in the U.S. go through air force training each year. Only 470 graduate as fighter pilots.

U.S. Air Force   military group that specializes in airplanes and jets

How Fighter Pilots Help

U.S. fighter pilots are stationed throughout the world. This means they can quickly respond to any emergency, such as an attack on U.S. property overseas. Many pilots and planes can then quickly reach trouble spots.

Anywhere in the world

Many fighter pilots live on air force bases. Others are stationed on **aircraft carriers**. These ships often hold 80 to 100 jets in a garage below deck.

Fighter fact!

Luke Air Force Base in Arizona covers 1.9 million acres (770,000 hectares). This one base is over half the size of Connecticut!

When there is trouble in any part of the world, the U.S. often sends aircraft carriers to the area.

aircraft carrier	huge ship with a deck where planes can take off and land
stationed	told to live and work somewhere

WHY TEAMWORK?

Fighter pilots rely on teamwork. Before **missions**, pilots are **briefed** on what their duties will be. They meet with **military** officers to study maps and mission details.

How to keep in touch

During a mission, a command leader watches a **radar** screen at a base or on another airplane. He or she will then tell a pilot if enemies are in the area.

Fighter planes fly in **formation** on their way to a target. The V-shaped group of planes keeps in contact with each other by radio.

Fighter fact!

When flying in formation, fighter jets are just 300 feet (91 meters) apart.

Command leaders oversee
a mission from base.

briefed	given the details about a task
formation	special pattern
mission	task or purpose
radar	technology that uses radio waves to locate an object

The threat of an F-15 Eagle's weapons, even if they are not used, helps make missions successful.

air refueling probe

20mm cannon

missile

ESCORTS

In some **missions**, U.S. fighter pilots serve as air **escorts**. Sometimes the escorts fly with Air Force One, the plane that carries the U.S. president.

Watching the ground

Pilots also escort vehicles on the ground. Recently, in Afghanistan, U.S. fighter pilots flew F-15s above trucks carrying food and medical supplies. This is because the U.S. **military** thought people might try to steal or destroy the supplies. Fighter pilots protected the supplies by flying over the area.

Fighter fact!

F-15 Eagles are the most common fighter plane. They have been in use since 1977.

escort	plane that goes with another plane or vehicle to make sure it is safe
refuel	to fill up with fuel again

Enemy radar cannot spot a stealth jet.

In 2003, F-117As flew in more than 100 U.S. missions in Iraq.

A New Kind of Fighter

In 1988 the **U.S. Air Force** started using a new kind of fighter plane. The F–117A Nighthawk is a **stealth** jet. It is perfect for top-secret spy **missions**.

A long flight

The F–117A is built to travel far. Nighthawks are piloted by members of the U.S. Air Force's 49th Fighter Wing. They are based at Holloman Air Force Base in New Mexico. With **refueling**, the planes can fly directly from that base to the war in Iraq, which is an eighteen-hour trip.

Fighter fact!

Exactly what makes the shell of the F-117A Nighthawk go unnoticed by radar is top secret.

stealth   aircraft designed not to be picked up by radar

The F-117A Nighthawk

Here are some details about the F-117A Nighthawk.

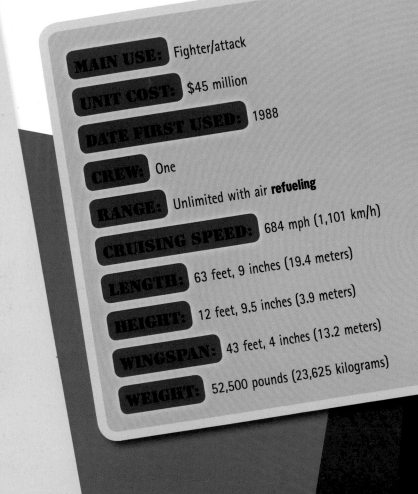

MAIN USE: Fighter/attack

UNIT COST: $45 million

DATE FIRST USED: 1988

CREW: One

RANGE: Unlimited with air **refueling**

CRUISING SPEED: 684 mph (1,101 km/h)

LENGTH: 63 feet, 9 inches (19.4 meters)

HEIGHT: 12 feet, 9.5 inches (3.9 meters)

WINGSPAN: 43 feet, 4 inches (13.2 meters)

WEIGHT: 52,500 pounds (23,625 kilograms)

Fighter fact!

An F-117A Nighthawk's mission plans are stored in a computer. Until the plane gets close enough for the pilot to see the destination, the plane is on autopilot.

autopilot — technology that automatically flies a plane without the pilot's help

HIGH-TECH

Fighter pilots are trained to use the most advanced technology. Sensors and cameras on the outside of the F–117A record information about the jet's surroundings. Pilots use this to look out for enemy planes.

What pilots need to know

Fighter pilots need a lot of information to fly a high-tech plane such as the F–117A Nighthawk. A **heads-up display** is used to **project** this information onto a screen in front of the plane's windshield. That way, pilots do not always need to look down to find the information they need.

heads-up display	system that gives a pilot information by showing it on a screen
project	to send out onto a surface
sensor	something that detects or records

An F-117A Nighthawk pilot watches a video of the ground below.

FLY UP

W

INS LIMIT

c 14

S 1010

Heads-up displays help pilots stay focused on the sky in front of them.

An F–16 Fighting Falcon can fly more than 500 miles (860 kilometers) to complete a mission.

Fighter fact!

The new F-16 helmets allow pilots to select a target in 1/25 of a second.

HITTING THE TARGET

Technology also helps fighter pilots identify targets.

How do special helmets help?

F–16 pilots use special helmets. The helmets show menu selections on the inside of the **visor**. The helmet can follow the pilot's eye and knows which item the pilot looks at. By looking at certain options, the pilot can select targets to fire upon.

At the same time, **infrared** cameras help fighter pilots detect enemy bases that may fire upon them. Fighter pilots need to react quickly to enemy fire.

infrared	method of seeing in the dark. It shows light from heat.
visor	clear part of a helmet that the pilot looks through

WAR MISSION

After a fighter pilot has located a target, he or she uses the plane's controls to get in position to fire.

How do pilots aim and fire?

Computers help fighter pilots to hit their targets. The pilot points out the target, and the plane's computers then make sure that the weapons are aimed correctly.

Once in position, a fighter pilot is able to fire heat-seeking missiles called sidewinders. These missiles locate the hot **exhaust** of an enemy plane.

Fighter fact!

As soon as the pilot has fired a missile, he or she can move on to the next target. The missile will keep going on its own, until it finds the target.

exhaust   gases that leave a plane's engines

Missiles on stealth jets are stored inside the plane.

Enemy planes often do not want to get into a battle with U.S. fighter jets.

SHOWING POWER

When enemy planes realize the power of fighter planes, they often **retreat**. However, the **mission** is not always over for the fighter pilot.

Enemy information

Fighter pilots also take part in **reconnaissance** missions. During these secret missions, pilots gather information about an enemy. The pilots look for enemy planes and tanks in the area. They also see how many enemy soldiers may be **stationed** near the weapons.

Fighter fact!

Fighter pilots use high-tech cameras to photograph enemy regions, even at night.

reconnaissance	search and exploration of enemy areas
retreat	to move away because you do not want to fight

MAINTENANCE

Mechanics check and fix planes when they return from a mission.

How to stay safe

After a mission, a plane lands on a base or an **aircraft carrier**. Mechanics check for any damage that may have occurred during the mission.

Different mechanics check different areas of the plane. Some mechanics work with the engines. Some work only with the fuel tanks. Others check the computer systems. These mechanics work to ensure that fighter jets are safe.

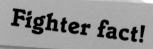

Fighter fact!

For every hour that a fighter jet spends in the air, mechanics and inspectors spend many hours checking that the plane is safe.

The work of mechanics helps fighter pilots keep the skies safe.

The F/A–22 Raptor (below) will replace the F–15 because it is faster and much more advanced.

An Important Job

Fighter pilots have an important role in the **military**. They are needed to get information about the enemy. They are needed to **escort** people on the ground and in the air. They are also needed to attack enemy forces.

What's the latest?

The **U.S. Air Force's** latest fighter jet is the F/A–22 Raptor. Like the F–117A Nighthawk, the F/A–22 Raptor is a **stealth** fighter. The plane was introduced in 2005, and it is the fastest jet in the U.S. military.

Fighter fact!

The F/A-22 Raptor can travel at about 1,522 miles (2,447 kilometers) per hour.

Glossary

aircraft carrier huge ship with a deck where planes can take off and land

autopilot technology that automatically flies a plane without the pilot's help

briefed given the details about a task

escort plane that goes with another plane or vehicle to make sure it is safe

exhaust gases that leave a plane's engines

formation special pattern

heads-up display system that gives a pilot information by showing it on a screen

infrared method of seeing in the dark. It shows light from heat.

military group of soldiers that fight to protect a country

mission task or purpose

project to send out onto a surface

radar technology that uses radio waves to locate an object

reconnaissance search and exploration of enemy areas

refuel to fill up with fuel again

retreat to move away because you do not want to fight

sensor something that detects or records

stationed told to live and work somewhere

stealth aircraft designed not to be picked up by radar

U.S. Air Force military group that specializes in airplanes and jets

visor clear part of a helmet that the pilot looks through

Want to know more?

Books

✷ Draper, Allison Stark. *Fighter Pilots: Life at Mach Speed*. New York: Rosen, 2001.

✷ Kennedy, Robert C. *Life as an Air Force Fighter Pilot*. New York: Children's Press, 2000.

✷ Lewis, Jon E., ed. *The Mammoth Book of Fighter Pilots*. New York: Carroll & Graf, 2002.

Websites

✷ www.aviation-history.com This is a site all about the history of flying.

✷ www.nasm.si.edu/ This is the website of the Smithsonian National Air and Space Museum.

If you liked this Atomic book, why don't you try these...?

Index